THE TALKING TREE AND OTHER STORIES

D1596726

The *Oxford Progressive English Readers* series provides a wide range of reading for learners of English.

Each book in the series has been written to follow the strict guidelines of a syllabus, wordlist and structure list. The texts are graded according to these guidelines; Grade 1 at a 1,400 word level, Grade 2 at a 2,100 word level, Grade 3 at a 3,100 word level, Grade 4 at a 3,700 word level and Grade 5 at a 5,000 word level.

The latest methods of text analysis, using specially designed software, ensure that readability is carefully controlled at every level. Any new words which are vital to the mood and style of the story are explained within the text, and reoccur throughout for maximum reinforcement. New language items are also clarified by attractive illustrations.

Each book has a short section containing carefully graded exercises and controlled activities, which test both global and specific understanding.

The Talking Tree
and Other Stories

David McRobbie

1992
Hong Kong
Oxford University Press
Oxford Singapore Tokyo

FRANKLIN PIERCE
COLLEGE LIBRARY
RINDGE, N.H. 03461

Oxford University Press

Oxford   New York   Toronto   Madrid
Kuala Lumpur   Singapore   Hong Kong   Tokyo
Delhi   Bombay   Calcutta   Madras   Karachi
Nairobi   Dar es Salaam   Cape Town
Melbourne   Auckland

and associated companies in
Berlin   Ibadan

© Oxford University Press 1992

All rights reserved. No part of this publication may be reproduced,
stored in a retrieval system, or transmitted,
in any form or by any means,
electronic, mechanical, photocopying, recording, or otherwise
without the prior permission of Oxford University Press

'Oxford' is a trade mark of Oxford University Press

Illustrated by Luk Wai Cheong

Syllabus designer: David Foulds

Text processing and analysis by Luxfield Consultants Ltd.

ISBN 0 19 585267 2

Printed in Hong Kong
Published by Oxford University Press,
18/F Warwick House, Tong Chong Street,
Quarry Bay, Hong Kong

CONTENTS

THE TALKING TREE

Zain's discovery

Zain was in the forest, looking for fruit. He was hungry. He sat under a tree and ate some of the fruit he had picked. When he got up to go home, he noticed that there was a hole at the bottom of the tree. He put his ₅ head inside the hole. He looked up. He could see the sky above. The tree was quite hollow. Zain pulled himself through the hole and stood up inside the tree. There was a smaller hole in the side of the tree. He could look out of it. ₁₀

'What a good hiding place,' he said aloud. 'No one can see me from outside.' His voice sounded strange inside the tree. It ₁₅ seemed much louder. It didn't sound the way it usually did. Zain decided to sing a song to hear his new voice. ₂₀

When he had sung the song, he decided to go home. But just then he heard someone talking outside. He knew the ₂₅ voice. It was Ali, a boy from his class at school.

'The singing came from here,' Ali said. 'But I can't see anyone, can you Abu?'

'No,' answered Abu. 'I don't think there is anyone else in this part of the forest.'

'You must obey me'

Then Zain spoke in a deep slow voice. 'Ali and Abu!' he said. 'What are you doing on my land?'

There was no answer for a minute. Then Zain heard Ali say in a frightened whisper, 'Who said that?'

'I am the Talking Tree,' said Zain. 'Everything in this part of the forest belongs to me. While you are here, you must obey me. If you do not, I shall come to your homes and take you away when you are asleep. Now, go and get me something to eat.'

'Yes, O Tree,' said Abu. 'We saw some fruit on our way here. We shall bring you some at once.' Zain heard the two boys run away along the path. He smiled as he waited for them to come back.

Ali and Abu ran back a few minutes later, with their hands full of fruit. They put the fruit at the bottom of the tree.

'Here is the food, O Great Tree,' said Abu. 'We hope you like it.'

'You have done well!' replied Zain. 'Now you may go home. But remember, you must not tell anyone about me or about this place. If you do, I shall change you into frogs. You must come back early tomorrow morning before you go to school and bring some more food for me. I shall want something to drink, too. Now you may go.'

Zain waited until Ali and Abu had gone. Then he came out of the tree. He was very pleased with himself. 'Ali and Abu will be angry if they discover who made

the tree talk,' he thought. 'They were very frightened!'
He laughed quietly.

Ali and Abu find out the truth

Next morning, Zain got up early and went back to the
hollow tree. It had rained a lot during the night and the
ground was wet and muddy. Zain stepped across the
mud and climbed inside his tree. He looked out through
the small hole in the side and waited for Ali and Abu.

A few minutes later, Ali and Abu came along the
path. They carefully put a bag of food and a cup at the
bottom of the tree. Zain spoke in his deepest voice.

'Thank you, boys,' he said slowly and loudly, 'You may
go to school now. But you must come again tomorrow.'

Ali and Abu walked away. But when they had gone
a little way, Abu stopped and held Ali by the arm. 'I
don't think that's a talking tree,' he said. 'Did you see
those marks in the mud near the foot of the tree? I think
someone was hiding there and tricking us.'

'No, I didn't notice,' said Ali. 'But let's hide and see
if anyone comes from that direction.'

A few minutes later, they saw Zain walking along the
path. He was carrying the bag of food and drinking
from Abu's cup.

'It's Zain!' whispered Ali in surprise. 'Shall we jump
out and frighten him?'

'No,' said Abu. 'I have a better idea. Come with me.'

A surprise for Zain

Abu ran quietly back towards the tree and Ali followed.
They looked carefully at the muddy marks and
discovered the hole at the bottom of the tree. Then they
guessed how Zain had tricked them.

That afternoon, when school had finished, Ali and
Abu looked in the forest for some wood, two long
pieces and some smaller pieces. They used these to
make a ladder. Then they hid the ladder in the long
5 grass near the hollow tree.

Next morning, Zain went to the tree again and
waited. Soon Ali and Abu appeared, carrying their
ladder.

'Good morning, O Great Tree,' said Ali. 'I have
10 brought some fruit juice for you today. I shall climb up
to the top of your tree and pour it in for you.'

'Hey! No! Don't do that!'
shouted Zain. 'Just put it at
the bottom of the tree.' But
Ali was already climbing
the ladder. He laughed as
he poured the juice
over Zain's head. Zain
coughed and cried as
the sticky drink went
into his nose and eyes.

Then Abu climbed the
ladder. 'I've brought you
some honey. Some insects
are still in it but I'm sure
they will obey you and not hurt you.'

'Help! No!' screamed Zain. But Abu was up the
ladder. He didn't really have any honey, but he did have
a big jar full of sticky yellow cooking-oil. He poured
30 the oil on Zain's hair. Zain tried to wipe it off, but it
was too sticky. He was covered with fruit juice and oil.
'Go away!' he shouted. 'You must never come near the
Talking Tree again.'

'All right, O Zain,' said Ali. 'We shall obey.' He and
35 Abu walked away through the forest, laughing loudly.

WHO CAN SAVE NOOR?

A little boy is lost

Harun was the smallest girl in Primary Five. She was
eleven years old, but she was no taller than the girls in
Primary Two. She was so small that she had to have a
special desk. The other desks were much too big.   5

Harun could read as well as the others in her class
and her writing was very neat. But she couldn't run fast
and she wasn't good at games. She was so small that
the big girls knocked her over when they ran after the
ball! The other girls and boys were very kind. They   10
always asked Harun to play. She knew she was too
slow, so she usually said she didn't want to.

Late one afternoon, she sat on the front step of her
home making a mat. She heard someone calling. She
looked up and saw a woman from the village walking   15
past the house. The woman looked very worried.

'Harun, have you seen Noor?' she asked. Noor was
the woman's little son. Harun knew him quite well.

'No,' she answered. 'He didn't come this way. Have
you lost him?'   20

'Yes. I left him playing near our house while I was
working inside,' she explained. 'When I went to get
him, he had gone. I must find him before night comes.'

'I'll help you,' Harun said. She put away her mat and
began to help the woman look for her son.   25

Too small to help

Soon nearly everyone in the village was looking for
Noor. They looked in the houses and in the gardens,

and some people went into the forest, calling loudly.
Several of the women stayed in the village to cook food
for the others and to help Noor's mother.

Night came and still no one had found the little boy.
5   The people returned for food. When they had eaten,
they decided to continue to look for Noor in the dark.
They went inside and got their torches.

The men said that the older
boys and girls could help. Harun heard
10   this and ran to get a torch. But when the men saw her,
they told her to go home again.

'No, Harun,' they said. 'You're too small to help. You
must stay at home with the smaller children.'

Poor Harun was very unhappy. She gave her torch
15   to a bigger girl and went home. From her window, she
watched the men and bigger boys and girls leave the
village. She saw the lights of their torches moving far
away among the trees.

Harun's idea

For a long time Harun lay in her bed and listened to the people calling to each other in the forest. She could not sleep. What had happened to Noor? Perhaps he had been bitten by a snake, she thought. She knew that there were dangerous snakes in the forest. Once, a woman had been killed by a snake when she went to gather wood.

Suddenly Harun remembered the well. She got up and ran outside. There was no one in the village, but she saw some lights far away in the dark. She ran towards them and saw a group of men walking back to the village. They looked tired and unhappy.

'Have you found Noor yet?' Harun called to them.

'Who's that? Oh, it's you Harun! No, we can't find him anywhere,' the men replied sadly.

'I have an idea!' Harun cried. 'Do you remember the old well? When I was a little child everyone in the village got their water from it.'

'Oh, yes, I remember it,' said one of the men. 'The top is covered with long grass and it is very hard to see now. Do you think Noor might have fallen in there?'

The men hurried away to look, with Harun running behind them. They ran down a little path. They had to push through some small trees before they came to the well. It was very narrow and one side had fallen in.

'Is he dead?'

'Quick! Point a torch down the well!' one of the men cried. The torch lit up the deep, narrow hole and there, at the bottom, lay the little boy.

'Noor, Noor! Are you hurt?' the men shouted. 'Noor!' But Noor did not answer. He did not even move.

'Is he dead?' Harun whispered.

'Perhaps he is,' one of the men replied, looking very worried. 'What can we do? The well is so narrow that none of us can go down it. We are too big,' he said,
5 looking at it again. 'How can we get Noor out?' The men thought hard.

Then Harun said quietly, 'I am very small.'

'But Harun, you aren't strong enough!' someone argued.

10 'I can do it,' she said. 'If you tie a rope around me and hold the end, I can go down the well. Then I can tie the other end of the rope around Noor too, and you can pull us both up.'

'I think she could do it,' said one of the men. He ran
15 back to the village to get a long rope.

Soon, they heard him running back through the trees.

'I've got the rope,' he shouted.

The other men took the rope. They tied it carefully around Harun and showed her how to tie it around
20 Noor. Then they held the other end and slowly put her down the well.

Mud and wet earth fell on Harun as she went down. She held her torch in her hand. Below, she could see Noor's small body.

25 **A proud and happy father**

It was wet at the bottom and the well was so narrow that she could hardly move. Noor did not make a sound and his body was cold. Harun tied the rope tightly around him. Then she called to the men, 'Pull
30 us up!'

Slowly the men pulled up the rope. Harun hoped that they would hurry. Noor was hanging, quite still, below her. Minutes seemed to pass. Then there was a

shout. Somebody held
her in their arms and took off
the rope. Suddenly, everybody was there.

'We've found Noor!'

'Harun saved him!' 5

'Where is he? Where is he? Is he all right?'

'He is still breathing. I think he has only hit his head,'
one of them cried thankfully. 'Quick! Let's take him to
the hospital.' The man hurried back to the village,
holding the little boy tightly in his arms. 10

When everybody was leaving, Harun felt a hand on
her head. She looked up and saw her father smiling at
her.

'You did well, Harun,' he said. 'None of the men
could have done it. I'm very proud of you.' 15

Harun and her father began to walk back along the
path. Harun smiled quietly. It was true. She had done
something that the men couldn't do and it was because
she was small! She was never unhappy again about
being the smallest girl in the class. 20

THE PETROL TANK

Horace's mistakes

Sam Bates owned a small boat-yard. The yard was quite close to a town. If you went about a mile along the river one way you would come to the town. If you went
5 six or seven miles the other way, you would get to the sea.

Twice every day the river water moved down the river, past Sam's boat yard, towards the sea. Twice every day it moved the other way. It went up the river, past
10 Sam's boat-yard, towards the town. Twice every day, when the tide changed, the water did not move in any direction for a while. At those times the water was still, and the river was quiet.

Sam was a very good worker. All the fishermen took
15 their boats to him to be repaired. He always did a good job, and he never asked them to pay too much money.

Horace worked for Sam, but Horace was not like Sam. He was not a very good worker. He did not know much about boats and he was always making mistakes.
20 Once he dropped a big, heavy hammer and made a hole in the bottom of a boat. Another time, he let a boat go away down the river. There was no one in it. The people had all got out. When they saw their boat in the middle of the river they shouted at Horace. Poor
25 Horace had to go after it in another boat to help them get it back. He felt very foolish.

One morning, Sam and Horace were busy painting an old boat. The sun was hot and it was very quiet by the river. Horace looked up. He could hear a motor in the distance. The sound got louder. Soon, Sam and Horace saw a small motor-boat coming down the river from the town. There was one man in the boat.

No oil in the petrol

The boat came to the boat-yard. The man stopped the motor, and got out. 5

'Do you sell petrol?' he called.

'Yes,' Sam answered.

'Then fill this, will you?' the man said. He handed a petrol tank to Sam.

'Horace!' Sam ordered. 'Fill this tank with petrol.' Horace took away the tank to fill it. He came back a few minutes later.

'I'm sorry I was slow,' he said. 'I've never put petrol 15 in a tank before.' Sam took the tank from Horace and gave it to the man in the boat. The man paid Sam. Then he started the motor. Sam pushed the boat away and it raced down the river towards the sea.

As they watched the boat disappear into the distance, Sam turned to Horace.

'You did mix the petrol properly, didn't you, Horace?' he said.

5   'What do you mean?' asked Horace.

'Did you mix oil with the petrol?'

'No,' Horace admitted.

Sam shook his head. 'Don't you know that you must mix oil with the petrol for motor-boats? If you don't do

10   that, the motor won't work properly. That poor man! His boat won't go very far! But it's too late to stop him now.'

Horace was sorry. Another mistake! The man would be very angry when his boat stopped. Horace went

15   sadly back to work.

A bank-robber

Later that morning they heard the sound of another motor. This time it was a car, a policecar. It stopped at the boat-yard and two policemen jumped out.

20   'Have any boats come down the river?' one of them asked. 'We are looking for a bank-robber.'

'A bank-robber!' Sam cried. He looked at Horace and then at the river.

'Yes,' said the policeman. 'A man went into the town

25   bank this morning with a gun. He said he would shoot the bank manager and he stole a lot of money. Then he ran out with the money and jumped into a car. We've been looking everywhere. A few minutes ago, we found the car near a bridge. We think he got into

30   a boat and came down the river.'

'Only one boat has passed here this morning,' said Sam, 'and I don't think it will go very far.' He told the policemen about Horace's mistake with the petrol.

'That must be the robber in the boat!' one of the policeman said. 'Let's go after him!' He jumped into one of Sam's boats.

The tide will turn

'You don't need to follow him,' Sam said slowly. The other men looked at him in surprise.

'What do you mean?' they asked.

'If we just sit down and wait, the robber will come back,' Sam said, smiling. 'We know the motor won't work properly. It has probably stopped already. The boat will keep going slowly down the river with the tide, but when the tide turns, the boat will come back here!'

'He's right!' said the policemen.

And he was right. Soon they saw a small shape appear far down the river. It was the motor-boat with the robber sitting in it. The motor had stopped and the boat was coming back towards them with the tide.

The policemen took another boat and went out to meet the robber. The robber was looking very angry.

As they led the robber away, the policemen called back to Horace, 'Thanks for your help, son!'

Sam and Horace laughed. Horace went back happily to work this time. He thought he was quite clever!

THE LOOK-ALIKES

Hassan and Ahmad

Once there were two cousins who lived in a village by the sea. Hassan was one year older than Ahmad but they looked exactly alike.

5   When they went to school, the teacher did not know which was Hassan and which was Ahmad. Hassan's mother then sewed a large 'H' on his shirt so that everyone would call him by the right name.

    Hassan and Ahmad soon discovered that they could 10   trick people. Sometimes Hassan pretended to be Ahmad and sometimes Ahmad pretended to be Hassan! Sometimes they changed shirts. No one knew which was which.

    Hassan and Ahmad grew up. They became young men and they still looked exactly alike. There was only one way to be sure about them. Hassan had a little mark on his left arm where a wild pig had once attacked him.

There were many pretty girls in the village and one of
them was Sharifa. Sharifa had wide brown eyes and a
nice shape. Hassan and Ahmad both wanted to marry
Sharifa. Sharifa was a quiet girl. She smiled at Hassan
and she smiled at Ahmad, but nobody knew which one   5
she liked best.

Wedding plans

One day Hassan went to see Sharifa's parents. He asked
them if he could marry Sharifa. When he left, Sharifa
ran off into the forest. She did not come back until it   10
was dark. When she came back, everyone could see
tears on her face. Soon the village people discovered
why she was unhappy. Sharifa did not want to marry
Hassan. She wanted to marry Ahmad.

Hassan was very sad and also very angry. But Ahmad   15
was very pleased. He told the village people that he
would marry Sharifa. Hassan ran away into the forest
and nobody could find him anywhere.

The village people began to make food ready for the
wedding feast. They picked the biggest fruit and chose   20
the best rice. They went out in their boats to catch fresh
fish. They killed some cows and the children happily
ran after chickens to catch them for the feast.

Very early on the morning of the wedding, Ahmad
went to the beach to look at one of his fishing-nets. As   25
he worked there, he saw someone running along the
sand towards him. He knew who it was at once. It was
Hassan.

'What are you doing here?' Ahmad asked.

'There is no time to explain,' said Hassan. 'Your father   30
is hurt. He is on the island.' Hassan pointed to an island
out across the sea.

Hassan's trick

'But I saw my father about an hour ago,' Ahmad said. 'He was in our house, making things ready for the wedding.'

5 'No, he's on the island,' Hassan repeated. 'He went over in his boat to get some birds' eggs for the feast. He slipped and fell on the rocks. So, quick! Let's go and help him.' The two young men hurried along the beach to another boat. They jumped in and rowed hard 10 until they reached the island.

'Where is my father?' Ahmad asked.

'He's along the beach near the bottom of the big rock,' Hassan said. 'You go to him. I'll pull the boat out of the water. Then I'll come and help you to carry him.' 15 Ahmad ran along the beach towards the big rock.

His father was not at the bottom of the rock. Ahmad looked around. There were not even any marks on the beach. No one had been there for a long time. Suddenly, he knew he had been tricked.

20 He turned and ran back towards the boat, but he was too late. Hassan was already rowing quickly back to the village.

Ahmad stood at the edge of the water and shouted out to Hassan. 'If I ever catch you, I'll kill you!'

But Hassan couldn't hear because of the noise of the wind and the waves. He kept on rowing as fast as he could towards the village.   5

Ahmed gets off the island

Ahmad waited for a long time on the island. He sat on the sand, sadly thinking about what was happening in the village. He couldn't try to swim back. The water was full of sharks. Ahmad had often seen them when   10
he was fishing. He could only wait for a boat to come past.

Several hours later, Ahmad knew it was time for the wedding feast to begin. Suddenly, he saw two men in a boat coming towards the island.   15

'Hey! Hey!' he shouted as loudly as he could. He jumped up and down, and waved his arms. The men were very surprised to see him there. They rowed in to the shore. 'It's Ahmad from the village next to ours!' one man said. 'What are you doing here? I   20
thought that you were being married today.'

'I am! I am!' Ahmad cried. 'Can you take me back in your boat? Please row as fast as you can. If you don't, I shall arrive too late.'

Ahmad jumped into their boat and the men began to   25
row. They rowed faster and faster. As they rowed, Ahmad told them what had happened.

In the village, the wedding feast had begun. But Sharifa was not happy. She did not know why.

Sharifa thought she was marrying Ahmad, but it was   30
really Hassan who sat beside her. Hassan was eating as much as he could. There was a big smile on his face. 'Soon I shall have Sharifa as my wife,' he thought.

'When Ahmad comes back, Sharifa and I will have left
the village!' He held out his hands for more pineapple.

Not too late

Suddenly Sharifa noticed something. Hassan looked at
5 her and she held his arm tightly.

'No, no!' Sharifa screamed. 'You are not Ahmad! I
don't want you as my husband! You are Hassan!' She
screamed and screamed and banged her head on the
ground. 'Where is Ahmad? Where are you hiding him?'
10 The village people all began to talk at once. 'What
did she say? What does she mean?'

'Look at the mark on his arm,' cried
Sharifa.

'She's right! She's
15 right! It is Hassan.
Where is Ahmad?'

Everyone pushed
forward. Some men held
Hassan and shook him so
20 hard that it hurt. No one
understood what had happened.
No one knew what to do.

Then suddenly there was a loud shout. Ahmad ran
through the trees towards Sharifa and held her in his
25 arms.

'Hassan, you are a bad man,' said Ahmad. 'A bad,
bad man!'

There was a lot more talking and shouting before
everyone understood. Then the people decided that
30 Hassan must leave the village for five years. Hassan went
away quietly, looking very sorry. Then the wedding
feast continued. Sharifa married Ahmad and they were
very happy together.

A NECKLACE OF WATER DROPS

A birthday every week

Many years ago, a Great King, called an Emperor, ruled China. This is a story about his daughter, the princess.

The Emperor was very rich, and he lived with his family in a large palace. The princess had her own rooms in the palace. She needed a lot of rooms because she owned so many things. The rooms were all filled up to the roof with her things. She liked receiving presents which cost a lot of money. Every time her father went away, he returned with a present for his daughter. If a visitor came to the palace, he always had to bring a present for the princess. Everyone in the country had heard about the princess who got everything she wanted.

When it was the princess's birthday, the Emperor always had to buy her a present. But this princess had a birthday every week! Everyone else has a birthday once a year.

'You had a birthday last week,' her father used to say.

'Did I?' she used to answer. 'That doesn't matter. I'll have another birthday this week.'

As the princess grew up, she collected more and more presents. She needed more and more rooms to keep them in. As soon as she got one thing, she thought of something else she wanted. She already had jewels and watches and toys and clocks of every kind.

One day she saw a fountain in the garden of a rich man. She watched the water shoot up into the air and splash down into a little pool. It looked beautiful,

especially when the sun shone on it. The princess went home and asked her father to give her a fountain. The Emperor told his servants to build one in the garden. They worked very
5   hard. When they had finished, the princess came to look.

The princess has an idea

'It really is beautiful!' she cried to her father. She looked at the bright, splashing water. A single drop of water
10   fell on her hand and ran down to her finger-tip. It stayed there for a few seconds, shining in the sun. She watched it with a soft smile on her face.

'Father,' she said, 'there is something else I should like.' The Emperor said nothing. 'I should like a lovely
15   new necklace to hang around my neck,' she continued.

'But you already have hundreds of necklaces,' the Emperor said.

'This one will be different,' replied the princess. 'What I want more than anything else in the whole
20   world, is a necklace made from drops of water.'

'Drops of water!' the Emperor repeated. 'But how can anyone make a necklace from drops of water?'

'I don't care how it is made,' the daughter answered. 'I want one. It is something I haven't got. I want to wear it around my neck the next time we have a great feast.' The Emperor was silent again.

Next day he sent his servants to bring him the best jeweller in the country.

'I want you to make a very special necklace for my daughter,' he told the jeweller. 'I want you to make a necklace of water drops.'

'But sir!' cried the jeweller. 'How can I do that?'

'I don't care how you do it.' The Emperor's head was aching. 'But start working!'

The jewellers go to prison

The jeweller went back to his shop and started to work. He collected many different kinds of string and then put some water in a big jar. He put his hand into the water and pulled it out. He let some of the drops on his hand fall on a piece of string. Then he did it again. But the drops fell off the string and splashed on the ground like tears. He tried using a different piece of string, but the same thing happened.

He tried again and again. He tried and tried to make the necklace, but he had to go back to the Emperor and tell him he could not do it. The Emperor was very angry. He wanted to punish the jeweller. He told his soldiers to throw him into the deepest, darkest prison in the palace.

'Bring me another jeweller! ' he cried.

But the next jeweller could not make a necklace of water drops. The soldiers threw him into the deepest prison in the palace, too.

'You will stay there until a jeweller makes a necklace
5   of water drops,' the Emperor roared. And he sent for more jewellers, and more. Soon the prison was full.

Then one day an old man walked into the palace.

'Are you a jeweller?' the Emperor asked.

'No, I'm a beggar,' the old man answered. 'But I've
10   heard about your problem.'

'Can you make a necklace of water drops?' the Emperor asked eagerly.

'Of course,' the old man replied. 'It's really quite easy. But I will need some help.'

15   'I am the Emperor,' the Emperor said. 'I can give you all the help you need. Tell me what you want and you shall have it.'

'I need a princess to collect the water drops for me,' the old man said. 'When the princess brings me the
20   water drops, I'll put them on a string for you. They'll look beautiful, I promise.'

The princess understands

The Emperor sent a servant to ask the princess to come. She listened to the old man and, smiling happily,
25   she ran off to the fountain. But when she returned, her hands were quite dry.

'It doesn't matter,' the old man said. 'Go back and get some more drops. I'll wait for you here.' The princess went back to the fountain and she collected
30   some more drops of water. But when she returned to the beggar, her hands were dry again. Then she understood that no one could make a necklace with drops of water. It was impossible.

'You silly girl!' said the beggar. 'If you can't collect the water drops, how can I make you a necklace?' The princess looked down.

'And how could all those jewellers make you a necklace?' the beggar went on. 'Silly girl!' he repeated and walked away.

The Emperor began to think about what the beggar had said. He knew then that he too had been silly.

He opened the prison and sent all the jewellers back to their homes. After that, the Emperor never gave his daughter any more presents. He even made her sell many of her best presents and send the money to the jewellers who had been shut in the prison.

The princess also gave many of her own things to the poor people of China. She became quite a good, kind person. And she only had one birthday each year, like everybody else.

6

SUI-MING'S BUSINESS

Sui-ming leaves school

Poor Sui-ming was very sad. It was raining heavily and he was hungry. His foot was hurting. His village was still two miles away. He sat down unhappily to rest.

5 Sui-ming looked back towards the town he had left that morning. He had been at school there for five happy years, but now that was finished. The headmaster had spoken to him in his office.

'The end of the year has come, Sui-ming, and it is 10 time for you to leave school,' the headmaster had said. 'You have learnt many things and I know you will be sad to go. But you are older than most of the other pupils and many younger children want to come here. We must make room for them.'

15 Sui-ming had said goodbye to his friends. He had picked up the few things that he owned. Then he had started the long walk back to his home. He remembered all this as he sat by the side of the road. His face was still sad as he got up and walked through the rain again.

20 Sui-ming was pleased to see his family when he arrived home, and they were pleased to see him. He helped his father in the garden. He cut wood for the fire and carried water for his mother. But he was soon tired of doing the same things every day. At night, he 25 sat in the house and talked with his parents. But there were no books in the house and the only radio in the village was broken. Sui-ming had an old bicycle, but one of the wheels was broken. He wished he had something else to do.

No eggs in town

One day, Sui-ming's father asked him to go to the town to sell some vegetables at the market. Sui-ming was pleased to go to town again. He climbed happily on to a market-lorry and it started along the road to the market.

There were a lot of people at the market and Sui-ming soon sold his vegetables. His mother had asked him to buy some sugar and tins of fish so Sui-ming went to look for the right shop. The shop was full of people too, and Sui-ming waited patiently. He heard two women talking near one of the shelves.

'The shop doesn't have any eggs,' one of the women said. 'I haven't seen any eggs in the town for weeks.'

'It's silly,' the other woman said. 'Someone could easily start a chicken farm near here. Then we should always have plenty of eggs.' The two women talked about this for a long time. They were quite angry because they could not buy any eggs. Sui-ming was thinking hard as he looked for a lorry to take him back to the village.

Sui-ming builds a farm

Next morning, Sui-ming counted twenty-two chickens that belonged to his mother and father. Often, they laid their eggs in the wood or in secret places where no one ever found them.

Sui-ming went into the forest and cut down branches from the trees to make a fence. He worked hard, making many posts for the fence and hammering them into the ground. Then he caught the chickens and put them inside the fence.

'Now I've got a chicken farm,' Sui-ming said. 'So hurry, chickens! Lay some
5 eggs for me to sell.'

But the chickens did not lay many eggs. Sui-ming was busy for the rest of the
10 week, collecting food for them and looking for eggs. After one week, he had filled only four boxes with very small eggs. He took them to town and sold them at a shop.

'They are very small eggs,' the owner said. 'Bring me
15 some big eggs and I'll pay you well for them.'

A visit to the Town Hall

Sui-ming was disappointed. He had worked hard but got very little money. He decided to ask someone about his chicken farm. He walked to the Town Hall and
20 asked to speak to someone who knew about farming. The man in the office was very friendly.

'You have a chicken farm,' he said. 'That's a good idea.'

Sui-ming asked how he could make his chickens lay bigger eggs.

25 'You must buy the right food for your chickens,' the man advised him. He told Sui-ming which food to buy and Sui-ming carefully wrote the name on a piece of paper.

'Then you must discover which chickens are not
30 laying eggs,' the man continued. 'This food is not cheap so you should not give it to chickens that don't lay eggs. You should buy some better chickens that will lay bigger eggs.'

Sui-ming asked where he could buy the good chicken food. The man told him the address of a place where he could buy better chickens. Sui-ming thanked the man and went home.

The happy chicken farmer

Slowly Sui-ming's chicken farm improved. Some of the village people sold their chickens to him and Sui-ming changed his old bicycle for ten more chickens. He fed them all with the best food. After one month the chickens were laying much bigger eggs.

'These are good, big eggs,' the shop-owner told him. 'I'll buy all the eggs you bring me.'

After three months, Sui-ming went to the airport and collected three big boxes. On the side of each box was written 'Best Chickens'. Sui-ming proudly carried them back to his farm.

Now Sui-ming had enough eggs to take to the shops in town every day. He also had to carry food back to the farm for the chickens. So, after a year, he decided to buy a new bicycle. One day, as he cycled to town with four boxes full of large fresh eggs, he suddenly remembered the day he left school. He had been so unhappy then. He wasn't unhappy now. He didn't have time to be! Sui-ming smiled to himself and began to whistle cheerfully.

THE ABRAHAM PRIZE

A special examination

'I have something very important to say,' said the teacher. The boys and girls in the class stopped working to listen.

5 'Next week, we shall have a special examination in English,' the teacher continued. 'The boy or girl who gets the highest mark will receive a prize. Many years ago, there was a boy at this school called William Abraham. That boy left school and became a doctor.

10 Now, every year, Mr Abraham gives a prize for the pupil who gets the best mark in a special English examination.'

'What is the prize, sir?' Wai-choy asked.

'The prize is good,' the teacher said. 'It is fifty dollars

15 to spend on books. The examination will be next Tuesday.'

The boys and girls were so excited by the news that the teacher had to order them to continue with their work.

20 On Tuesday morning everyone was ready for the examination. Most of the boys and girls had done some work for the examination at home.

'Your examination papers are on your desks,' the teacher said. 'You must not cheat. If anyone copies

25 his neighbour's work, I will not let him continue the examination. You may begin now.' The boys and girls started work. They had to answer twenty questions in one hour.

'You are cheating, Wai-choy,'

Wai-choy looked at his paper. The first few questions looked quite easy but there were some harder ones near the end of the paper. He picked up his pencil and began to write.   5
  Wai-choy finished the fifteenth question. He looked at the classroom clock. It was twenty minutes to twelve. There was not much time left. He started   10
work on the sixteenth question.
Just then, a piece of folded paper landed on his desk. Wai-choy
looked around. He saw Ying-kee biting the end of his pen and looking at him. Wai-choy opened the note and   15
read: 'What is the answer to Question Eleven?'
  Wai-choy looked angrily at Ying-kee and shook his head. He folded the note and threw it back.
  'What are you doing, Wai-choy?' the teacher asked.
'Give me that piece of paper!' The teacher picked up   20
the note from Ying-kee's desk. He opened it and read the message inside.
  'You are cheating, Wai-choy,' he said.
  'No, sir, ...' Wai-choy began to say.
  'But I saw you throw this note,' the teacher said.   25
  'But sir, I ...' said Wai-choy.
  'I told you not to cheat,' the teacher said. 'Give me your paper and go outside, Wai-choy. I won't let you finish the examination.'

An accident   30

Wai-choy was very unhappy. He walked out of the classroom with tears in his eyes. He took his bicycle

from the hut and rode out of the school yard. He cycled along the road with his head down, thinking about his bad luck. Then he looked up suddenly and saw an old man right in front of him. Crash! Wai-choy and the old
5 man both fell over on the road. Wai-choy jumped up and helped the old man to stand. The old man did not seem to be hurt.

'I'm very sorry, sir,' Wai-choy said. 'I wasn't looking.'

10 'And I was walking on the wrong side of the road,' the old man replied. 'So we both made silly mistakes. And I'm not hurt.' The old man looked kind and his smile was friendly. Wai-choy liked him.

'And why are you not in school?' the old man asked.
15 'It's not time to go home yet, you know.'

'I was sent out of my class,' Wai-choy explained. Soon, he was telling the old man all about Ying-kee's note. The old man listened patiently.

'Can you prove that you didn't write the note?' he
20 asked. 'If you can prove it, then the teacher will listen to you.' Wai-choy shook his head.

'No, I don't think that I can,' he said. Just then he noticed a pen in the old man's pocket.

'Wait a minute!' he cried. 'I think I can prove that I
25 didn't write it. The note was written with a pen. I was writing my answers to the examination with a pencil.

I don't have a pen. Thank you for making me think about it. Now I can show my teacher that what I said was true! I must go back.' Wai-choy got on his bicycle and quickly rode back to school.

Wai-choy proves he was telling the truth 5

The teacher was in the classroom, reading the examination papers when Wai-choy arrived.

'I didn't think you would cheat in the examination, Wai-choy,' he said.

'But I didn't cheat,' Wai-choy said. 'That note was 10 written with a pen and I always use a pencil. I don't have a pen. Look at my answers. They are all written with a pencil.'

The teacher picked up the note and looked at it.

'Someone else threw that note,' Wai-choy said. 'I was 15 throwing it back when you saw me.'

'Can you prove this?' the teacher asked.

'The note asks for the answer to Question Eleven,' Wai-choy said. 'I had finished Question Eleven so why should I want to know the answer?' The teacher looked 20 at Wai-choy's examination paper.

'Yes, you had finished Question Eleven,' he agreed. 'And your answer is correct.'

'If you look at the writing in the note, you will see that it is not the same as my writing,' added Wai-choy. 25 The teacher looked first at the note and then at Wai-choy's examination paper. He looked up.

'Wai-choy, I have made a mistake. Please forgive me,' he said. 'Who threw the note?'

'I'm sorry,' Wai-choy answered. 'I can't tell you.' 30 The teacher smiled.

'That was a silly question,' he said. 'I didn't think you would answer it. All right, Wai-choy. Sit down. You may have twenty minutes to finish the examination.' Wai-choy smiled and sat down to finish Question Sixteen.

Two prize-winners

A few days later the teacher told the class the results
5   of the examination.

'Two pupils share first place,' the teacher said. Everyone waited to hear the names of the two pupils. 'One is Kwai-yin who had eighty-nine marks.' The boys and girls clapped their hands loudly.

10   'Wai-choy also had eighty-nine marks,' the teacher continued. 'So Kwai-yin and Wai-choy must share the Abraham Prize.' The boys and girls clapped again.

'Mr Abraham will come to the school this afternoon to give the prize,' the teacher said.

15   That afternoon, Wai-choy was surprised to discover that Mr Abraham was the old man whom he had knocked over with his bicycle. Mr Abraham laughed when he gave Wai-choy his share of the prize.

'I think that you must have been able to prove your
20   story,' he said as they shook hands.

'Yes, I proved it, all right,' Wai-choy said with a happy smile. And he went back to his seat with his share of the Abraham Prize.

NICOLAS AND ABSALON

A husband for Alice

Once, there were two young men named Nicolas and Absalon. They were quite different from each other. Nicolas worked in a shop. He was clever, but very lazy. Absalon worked in a small workshop. He was good at 5 making things out of metal. He was a silent young man, but he worked hard and he earned quite a lot of money.

Both of these young men wanted to marry the same girl. Her name was Alice and she lived in a house quite near Absalon's. Absalon often saw her as she walked 10 past the open door of his workshop. Sometimes she smiled at him. Absalon was always a little sad when he saw her.

'Alice would be a good wife for me,' he said in his slow way. 15

Alice's father didn't want her to marry either Absalon or Nicolas.

'I want you to marry a man who is rich and clever,' he told his daughter. 'Don't waste your time thinking about those two. Find a husband who is rich and 20 clever.' Nicolas was clever but he wasn't rich. Absalon was rich but he wasn't clever. Alice's father refused to let the two young men come to the house. Alice didn't care about Absalon but she did care about Nicolas.

The dream 25

Absalon sadly stopped hoping to marry Alice. But Nicolas made a plan.

One morning, Alice and her father were out walking. They saw Nicolas coming towards them. He was carrying some long pieces of wood. They looked very heavy.

5   'Where are you going with all those planks, young man?'asked Alice's father. Nicolas put the planks down and wiped his face with his hand.

'It's a long story,' he began. 'My father had a dream a few nights ago. In his dream he saw a great flood. It 10 rained and rained for a whole week without stopping. Water from the rivers got higher and higher. The water began to flow fast all over the land. It broke down bridges and washed the roads away. Cows, sheep, pigs and horses fell into the water and were drowned. Many 15 homes were destroyed. Hundreds of people were killed. It was horrible!'

Alice's father was very interested. 'But where are you taking the wood?' he asked.

'We're going to build a boat,' Nicolas continued. 'This 20 boat will save our lives. We'll build it on the roof of our house and, when the flood water rises, we'll sail away and be saved.'

'Do your father's dreams always come true?' Alice's father asked.

'Yes,' Nicolas said. 'They always come true. Every morning I say to my father, "What did you dream last night, father?" and he tells me. That's how I know what is going to happen. But I must go home with this wood. We haven't much time before the flood comes.' Nicolas   5
picked up the planks and carried them home.

Alice's father is busy

Alice's father was silent on the way home. He was thinking about the dream. By the time they arrived, he had decided.   10

'I'll build a boat too!' he cried.

Later that afternoon, some men came to his house carrying some long planks, and a big box of nails. Alice's father started work at once. He fetched a ladder and carried the wood up to the roof. Then he carried   15
up his tools and started to build the boat.

He worked all day. Even when night came, he kept on working. He wanted to be ready when the flood came.

'Bang! Bang! Bang!' went the hammer as Alice's father   20
nailed planks together.

Alice sat in her bedroom and listened to the hammering on the roof. Just then, she heard someone whistle softly. She saw Nicolas standing outside in the dark.   25

'My plan is working,' he whispered. 'Your father is too busy to think about us. Now we can arrange to run away and get married.

'I'll come back in an hour's time,' Nicolas continued. 'While I'm away, you must collect the things you will   30
need. When I come back, you can climb down the ladder and we can go away together.' Alice agreed to his plan.

Jealous Absalon

They did not see a man hiding in the trees near the house. It was Absalon. He had heard them talking and he was very angry and jealous.

5 'So they're going to run away together,' he said to himself. 'I'll spoil their plan!' He went to his workshop to get something.

Just then, it began to rain. At first, only a few drops fell. Then heavier drops began falling fast from the
10 cloudy sky.

The rain fell on Alice's father up on the roof.

'Rain!' he said to himself. 'That dream was right! This must be the beginning of the flood.' So he worked even harder. 'I must finish this boat,' he said as he
15 hammered another nail into a plank.

An hour later, Nicolas came to Alice's window. By this time, it was raining heavily.

'I'm ready, Nicolas,' Alice called softly. 'I've put my clothes in a bag. Please come up the ladder and carry
20 them for me.' Nicolas climbed up the ladder and took the bag from Alice. He started to climb down again.

A painful wedding present

At the bottom of the ladder, Absalon was waiting. He was wet and angry and very jealous. And in his hands
25 he held a large spade that he had brought from his workshop. It was red hot.

'This is a wedding present for you!' Absalon shouted, as he put the red-hot end of the spade against Nicolas's trousers.

30 'Help!' Nicolas screamed. 'I'm burning. I need water! Water!' Nicolas ran to a nearby fish-pond. Smoke and fire were coming out of his trousers. He jumped into the water with a loud splash.

Up on the roof, Alice's
father heard someone
shouting 'Water!' Then he
heard a splash.

'The flood has come!' he shouted. 5
'And I have just finished my boat!' He threw down his
hammer and pushed the boat off the roof. It slid down
and over the edge. Alice's father waited to hear the
splash as it landed in the water. But he heard only a
crash and a loud scream. The boat had landed on 10
Absalon!

The story ended sadly for everyone. Nicolas couldn't
sit down for a month. Absalon's leg was broken. Alice
is still looking for a husband who is rich and clever,
and her father is still angry about building a boat for a 15
flood that did not come!

WILLIAM AND THE STRANGE TOYS

Visitors from space

William drove his van along the road. It was a nice, bright day and he sang as he drove. His van was carrying a lot of new toys from the toy factory. He was
5 taking them to a big shop in the town. William enjoyed going to the toy factory and he liked to see the new toys before they were put into his van. He was always surprised at the new kinds of toys that the factory made.

As he drove along, the engine of the van began to
10 make strange noises. It began to cough and spit. Then it went, 'Ka-chonk, ka-chonk, ka-chonk!' And then it stopped. William soon discovered what was wrong. There was no petrol in the van's petrol tank. He had forgotten to fill it.

15 'It doesn't matter,' he said. 'It's a nice day for a walk.' And he set off down the road to get some petrol.

Far up in the sky, there was a small silver circle. It flew round and round slowly. It came lower and lower. Then it landed on the ground near the van. It was a
20 flying saucer!

Unfriendly people

There were two spacemen in the flying saucer and they had come from another world. They opened the door of the flying saucer and climbed out. They saw the van
25 standing at the side of the road.

'Perhaps we shall find some people in this strange thing,' one of the spacemen said in his own strange language. They looked around the van but they did not see anyone. Then they opened the back door of the van and climbed inside. They saw all the boxes and opened one on which 'Baby Dolls' was written. Inside the box, there were several dolls.   5

'There are some people in here!' one spaceman cried.

'And they are the same size as we are,' said the other spaceman. 'Good morning, how are you?' he said to the dolls. The dolls said nothing.   15

'We have come from another world to meet you,' the first spaceman explained. But the dolls did not move or speak.

'They are not very friendly,' said the second space-man sadly. Just then, the spacemen heard someone   20 whistling outside the van. They looked out and saw William carrying a tin of petrol.

'Another person is coming,' cried the first spaceman. 'He is much bigger than these people.'

'But he looks friendly,' the second spaceman said.   25

Wonderful toys

William saw that the door of the van was open.

'Who opened that door?' he asked himself. Then he saw the spacemen standing up in the back of the van. 'How did these dolls get out of their boxes?' he said.   30 'Something strange is going on here.' He pushed the two spacemen into the box and shut it hard. Just then, he saw the flying saucer on the ground near the van.

'Someone has taken a toy out of the van!' he said in surprise. 'This is very strange.' He picked up the flying saucer and put it in the back of the van too. By this time, the two spacemen had climbed out of the box.

5   'These two dolls are out of the box again,' William said and picked them up. The two spacemen fought and shouted.

'What wonderful toys,' said William. 'They can walk about and they can make noises. They must work by
10   electricity.' So he tried to switch off the electricity. He twisted their noses and pushed their stomachs and pulled their arms. But they just kept on calling out and fighting.

William did not want to waste any more time. He
15   pushed the spacemen back into the box and shut it again. Then he shut the door of the van. He poured petrol into the tank, started the motor, and drove away.

The flying van

The spacemen did not like being in the box. William
20   was driving along a very rough road and the dolls were rolling around and falling against them.

'They are all unfriendly people!' the spacemen cried. They fought, and pushed, and managed to open the box. They saw their flying saucer. They jumped in and
25   started the engine. They were very pleased that it still worked.

The spacemen flew around inside the van, looking for a way to get out. They decided to fly up and break through the roof of the van. The flying saucer had a
30   very strong engine but the roof was strong too. Soon the flying saucer had lifted the van off the road. A few seconds later, it was flying through the air like an aeroplane!

William was very surprised. He felt the van going up into the air. He saw the road getting smaller below him. He could see the tops of the trees. He looked down and saw all the cars and lorries on the road below. Then he was inside a large cloud. 5

'That's very strange,' he said. 'No one told me that this van could fly! Perhaps that was aeroplane petrol that I put in the tank!' The van went on flying, and William became worried.

The two spacemen were worried too. They did not 10 know how to get out of the van. But then, their flying saucer hit the handle of the back door. The door opened and the spacemen flew out. They flew up and away while the van began to fall back to the ground.

On top of a mountain 15

Luckily, there was a mountain right under the van so that it did not fall far. It landed with a loud crash. The wheels fell off and bounced away down the mountain in different directions. William got out to see if there was anything wrong with the van. Then he began to 20 walk slowly down the mountain to find people who would help him.

The spacemen flew back to their own world. As they went, they spoke to their leader by radio.

'There are two kinds of people in the other world,' 25 they reported. 'There are big people and small people. And both kinds are very unfriendly!'

Down below, William was still worried. He had found a telephone and he was going to telephone the manager of the toy factory. He wanted to tell him what 30 had happened. But he didn't know how to explain that the van had crashed on the top of a mountain!

THE DRAGON OF TUMALUMA

An unhappy place

The island of Tumaluma was beautiful. There was always
plenty of fruit on the trees. There were always lots of
nice vegetables growing in the fields. Many different
5   kinds of fish swam in the blue sea, and they were mostly
very good to eat. There was no fighting and the people
did not often argue. But Tumaluma was an unhappy
place because the people were always afraid.

The people were afraid of the dragon that lived on
10   the island. Each day, as they went to work in their
fields, the people looked around to see if the dragon
was anywhere near. When the men went fishing, they
shut their wives and children in their houses so that the
dragon would not see them.

15   At night, the dragon sometimes slid down from the
hills where it lived. The people in the village were
often woken up by the sound of wood breaking.
Sometimes there was a crash as the dragon pushed over
a neighbour's house. There was a lot of noise and
screaming in the dark, and then silence. The people
stayed awake for the rest of the night, listening in
fear. In the early morning, they went outside.
Usually, they found that one or two houses had
been pushed to the ground. The people in
them had disappeared.

The people tried to kill the dragon several times. Once, five men had gone to fight it. But the dragon was too strong and quick, and all five men had died. Next, the people had dug a big hole in the ground to catch the dragon. But the dragon had slid around it. 5 Then, they had sharpened the end of a large tree and attacked the dragon with this. But the dragon had broken the tree easily. So the men decided to leave Tumaluma.

Alone on the island 10

The men put their wives and children and all their things into boats. Everyone was busy. Soon everyone was ready to begin the journey across the sea

There was a young woman living on the island with her little son, Tara. The boy was only three years old. 15 The woman's husband had died. She was a widow. She was too poor to have her own boat, and there was no one to take her and Tara away.

'Please take us with you!' she cried out.

'I can't,' each man replied. 'If I take you, I shall have 20 to throw out some of my things. We don't know when we shall find another island, so we can't leave behind our food or our fishing-nets.' The woman ran along the beach, stopping at each boat and asking the men to take her. But each man shook his head sadly and 25 turned away.

The people rowed away from the island in their boats. They looked back and saw the woman standing on the beach with her young son in her arms. The men were sorry for her, but they rowed even harder until 30 they could see her no longer. When night came, they had already forgotten about the poor widow and her child.

Tara grows older

The woman cried when the boats left the island. When night came she did not want to stay in any of the houses. She found a cave to sleep in, but she could not
5   light a fire because the dragon might see the smoke. She was cold and unhappy, lying all night in the cave with her small son.

Next day, the widow took her son to another cave high up in the mountains. They lived there together for
10   several years. The widow and Tara never cooked their vegetables or fish. The mother never showed Tara how to light a fire, and she never lit one, because the dragon might see the smoke. Sometimes she saw the dragon lying asleep on the beach or in the empty village.

15   Tara became stronger as he became older. His mother showed him many things. He learnt how to hunt the pigs on the island. He learnt how to dive for fish. His mother also told him why the people had left the island.

When he heard the story, Tara began to hate the
20   dragon. He made many plans to kill the great animal. He began to follow it and watch it. The dragon still did not know that Tara and his mother were on the island. When the boy was twelve years old, he discovered how to make fire. He was pleased with his discovery. Now
25   he knew how to kill the dragon!

The dragon eats stones

Tara collected some heavy stones and placed them at the top of a hill. Then he collected lots of dry grass and sticks, and he put these around the stones. He lit the grass and sticks. Soon they were burning fast, with tall 5 hot flames. Smoke rose high into the air. Tara cut a long, thick stick for himself, and waited.

Far down on the beach, the dragon smelt the smoke. It knew that fire was made by people. It had not eaten people for many years. It began to slide up the hill to 10 discover where the smoke came from.

The dragon saw the boy standing at the top of the hill near the big fire. It moved forward with its mouth wide open and its long red tongue flashing in and out. Tara used his long stick to push one of the stones down 15 the hill into the dragon's open mouth.

The stones had been in the middle of the fire and they were red-hot. The dragon swallowed the first one. Tara pushed another stone down and the dragon swallowed that one too. Another stone crashed down, 20 and another. The dragon's great body became heavy and the hot stones began to hurt its stomach. The dragon roared in pain. Then it started to roll down the hill. It rolled faster and faster, knocking down trees and crashing against rocks. It rolled onto the beach 25 and across the sand. Then it rolled into the sea and disappeared under the water in a great cloud of steam.

The people come back

Tara dived into the water and cut off the dragon's head. He and his mother put the head on a big piece of wood and let it float away across the sea. That night, they lit
5 a fire and cooked a meal, for the first time in many years.

The dragon's head floated across the sea on the piece of wood for many days. Then it landed on the island where the people of Tumaluma now lived. When the
10 people saw the head, they knew that the dragon was dead. They put their things into their boats and sailed back to Tumaluma.

Tara and his mother were pleased to see their people again. They told the story of Tara's fire and the red-hot
15 stones. Everyone thought Tara was very brave. A few years later, they chose him to be their king. He ruled for many years.

If you go to Tumaluma today, you can still see the stones that Tara used to kill the dragon. The people of
20 the island will tell you the story. But you know it already.

ELIWUNAO

Two bad boys

Naime and Harao hated school work. They tried very hard not to do it. During lessons they whispered and laughed together so much that the teacher made them sit in opposite corners of the class room. 5

One day, Naime threw a note to Harao. It said:

Dear Haraw,
after scool we ken hev sum fun. I got a good idia. Meat me behine the tool stor en don tel aniwon.

Your firend Naime. 10

Harao read the note slowly. He couldn't read very well. Then he turned to look at Naime and nodded his head.

After school the boys met behind the tool store. This was a little building where the school gardener kept 15 his tools.

'I found a big box on the road this morning', Naime said. 'I hid it in the long grass.'

'What's in the box?' Harao asked.

'I don't know', Naime replied. 'Let's go and find out.' 20

The boys went out of the school yard and ran along the road until they came to some long grass. Naime showed Harao the box.

'Come on. Let's open it'. Harao said. They started trying to open the lid of the box. It was hard work. 25 After a while they broke the lid with a large stone. Inside, they found a lot of long thin round things.

A word they cannot read

'It's only a box of candles!' Naime said.

'Candles?' asked Harao.

'Yes. You know, you use them
5 to light your home with when
the electricity goes wrong.'
He picked one up to look
at it more closely. 'I was
hoping it would be a box
10 of watches or radios or
something like that.'

'Well, we can take them
home and use them at night,'
Harao said. 'Our parents will
15 be very pleased. They will
save a lot of money.'

He looked at the side of the box. There was a long
word there, printed in big red letters. 'What does that
word mean?' he asked.

20 Naime looked at it for a long time. Then he shook
his head. 'I can't read it very well,' he said slowly. 'It's
not a word we've learned at school.'

'Get out of the way and let me read it,' Harao said.
He gave Naime a push. Then he looked at the word
25 for a long time, too, but he couldn't read it either. He
tried to pronounce the word. 'The first letter is E, I
think,' he said, ' and the second letter is L, and the third
letter is I.'

The two silly boys didn't know it, but they were
30 looking at the word upside down. This is what they
saw:

E L I W U N A O

They both tried to pronounce the word and then at
last Naime cried out: 'I know! It's "Eliwunao"!'

A good hiding place

Harao was silent. He scratched his head. 'What are eliwunaos?' he asked at last. Naime looked at him.

'This is what an eliwunao is,' he said, picking one up from the box and waving it under Harao's nose. 'They're just candles. Come on, let's hide them somewhere. I know a good hiding place.' They picked the box up and carried it back to the school yard.

There was a large pile of leaves in one corner of the school yard near the gardener's tool store. They hid the box under the leaves, and then they went home.

Every day, lessons began with question time, so, next morning, Harao asked his teacher what the strange word meant.

'I've never heard of it Harao,' he said. 'Come out and write the word on the blackboard please.' So Harao went to the blackboard and slowly and carefully printed the word in large letters. He said that he had seen the word written on the side of a box. But the teacher still could not tell him what the word meant.

The teacher understands

Then it was time for morning news. One boy told the class that the people in his village were going to build a new sports ground. A girl told the class that the police were looking for a box of dynamite. The box had been stolen from the back of a truck. The children talked about the news for a while. Then they took out their English books and started to do some writing.

As they worked, the teacher looked at the word on the blackboard. He wrote something on a sheet of paper and turned the sheet around until it was upside down. Then he put the paper in front of Harao.

'Is that the word that you saw on the box?' he asked.

'Yes sir,' Harao said. 'That's the word. Eliwunao.'

Slowly the teacher turned the sheet of paper around.

'This word says "dynamite," the teacher said. 'It is
5 very dangerous. What did you do with it?'

'We hid it, sir,' Harao answered.

'Where?' the teacher asked.

'Under that pile of leaves, sir,' Harao said, pointing
out of the window to the corner of the school yard.
10 Everyone looked out of the window and there they saw
the old school gardener standing next to the pile of
leaves. He had just set fire to them
and they were burning brightly.

The boys learn to read

15 The teacher looked horrified. He hurried to the window
and opened it.

'Run for your life,' he roared.

'What did you say, sir?' the old man shouted back.
He was very old and he could hardly hear anything.

'I said RUN!' the teacher roared again. The old man understood that something was wrong, and he ran.

'Everyone get under your desks!' the teacher ordered. There was a lot of talking and laughing as the boys and girls got under the desks. Suddenly there was a great crash, louder than the loudest thunder. The dynamite had exploded. The building shook, pictures fell off the walls, the windows rattled, the doors burst open. There were leaves and dust and small pieces of glass everywhere. Luckily, no-one was hurt. The old gardener was shaking with fright. His wheelbarrow was in pieces. The tool store had disappeared.

For the next hour, it seemed that everyone in the world had come to visit the school. The police were there and so were the firemen and several ambulances. Everyone had something to say to Naime and Harao. The police asked them questions about finding the box. The firemen told them how dangerous dynamite was. The teacher told them how silly they were not to be able to read properly. There was a long line of people who wanted to say something to Naime and Harao.

All that happened last year. Now, Naime and Harao are the two best students at reading in the school. If anyone says 'eliwunao' to them, they just stick their heads in their books and keep very quiet.

THE CONCERT

The piano player

One Wednesday morning, Peter and his sister Neri
walked into the school yard. A small crowd of children
were standing around the notice board. Peter and Neri
5 joined the crowd and read the new notice.

'There's going to be a school concert, Peter,' Neri
said. 'See, the notice says, "All children who want to
sing or play in the concert must tell the headmaster
today or tomorrow".' Just then Wili and Grace joined
10 the crowd. Wili and Grace were Peter and Neri's friends.
They were all in Primary Five.

'I think I'll sing some songs.'
Grace said.

'I'll play my flute,' Wili
15 said. 'What can you
play, Peter?' he asked.

'I can play football,'
Peter said. Everyone
laughed.

20 'I don't mean that kind of playing,' Wili said.

'Oh, I can play something,' Peter said. He thought
carefully, and then said. 'Er, yes. I can play the piano.'

'That's wonderful, Peter,' Grace said.

'But there isn't a piano in the school,' Peter said,
25 smiling. 'So I won't be able to play at the school
concert.'

'The headmaster borrowed a piano yesterday,' Wili
told Peter. 'So you can play after all.' Peter's face
changed. He did not reply.

Peter can practice

Just then the headmaster came along.

'Good morning, boys and girls,' he said. 'What are you going to do in the school concert?'

'Peter's going to play the piano,' Grace said.   5

'I didn't know you could play the piano, Peter,' the headmaster said.

'I'm not very good, Mr Thompson,' Peter said quickly. 'I haven't practised for a long time.'

'You can practise on the piano that I borrowed for the   10
concert,' the headmaster said, and he went to his office.

The children moved away.

'You can't play the piano, Peter,' Neri said when Wili and Grace had gone.

'I know,' said Peter sadly. 'I only said I could play it   15
because everyone else was going to do something in the concert. Now I'm really in trouble!'

'What are you going to do?' Neri asked.

'I'll think of something,' Peter answered.

The plan   20

At lunch time Peter and Neri went to the headmaster's office. Peter had a plan. He explained it to Neri as they walked along.

'I saw the headmaster going to lunch,' Peter said. 'We can go into his office and borrow his cassette player.   25
We can record some piano music from the radio. At the school concert, you can hide the recorder behind the piano. When the time comes for me to play you can switch it on. When the people hear the music they will think I'm playing.' Neri was not very sure about the   30
plan, but she decided to help.

'Well, it might work,' she said. 'Let's try it.'

They went into the headmaster's office and found the cassette player. Neri switched on the radio and Peter put the cassette player near it. They waited until some piano music started, then they switched on the cassette
5   player. Neri and Peter left the room to have some lunch.

'We can come back in a few minutes and switch the cassette player off,' Peter said.

10   They passed Wili and Grace outside. Wili and Grace were carrying brooms. They looked very cross. 'I think someone has told them to do some cleaning,' Neri said.

Peter and Neri came back ten minutes later and switched off the cassette player. Peter was feeling very
15   pleased with himself.

Beautiful music

On the night of the concert, Neri hid the cassette player behind the piano. The headmaster and some of the teachers sat in the front row. The children sang songs
20   and played the guitar or the flute. Each time the audience clapped loudly at the end. At last it was Peter's turn.

Neri knelt behind the piano and switched on the cassette player. Peter moved his hands up and down and pretended to play. The music was very beautiful and the audience thought Peter was a wonderful piano player. Peter kept playing. He had a happy smile on 5 his face. But then the music stopped. 'Some silly person left the radio playing!' said a voice. It was Wili. His voice was coming from the cassette player. Then Grace's voice said angrily, 'Why did the headmaster tell us to clean his dirty old office? Let's brush the dirt 10 behind this cupboard.'

Peter looked very surprised. He stopped moving his hands. The headmaster was staring at Peter. Wili was looking at Grace. Grace was looking quite ill. The audience roared with laughter. 15

'Peter and Wili, Neri and Grace!' the headmaster said in a voice like thunder. 'I'll see you all in my office tomorrow morning.'

The audience thought it was the best part of the whole concert. They talked about it for weeks. The four 20 friends didn't forget it for a long time either.

13

DON'T GO NEAR THE WHARF:
PART ONE

A strange story

Piren and Serina were on their way to town. Their
mother had asked them to buy the local newspaper
and some fish at the market. They enjoyed going to
5 town because there was always something interesting
to see. But they liked going to Tom Barata's shop best.

Tom Barata sold newspapers, books and toys. He
also sold all kinds of things for writing, like stamps,
writing-paper, pens and pencils.

10 There was a small printing machine at the back of
the shop. Every week, Tom Barata and his wife printed
the local newspaper. When it was printed, they sold it
in their shop. The people in the town liked reading
local news. It was about their own town, and about

15 people they knew. Many of them
bought the newspaper.

Serina and Piren bought the
newspaper for that week, and
looked at the toys. Then they

20 left the shop to go to the
market to buy the fish. As
they walked along, Serina
looked at the newspaper.

'Is there any interesting
25 news this week?' Piren asked.

'Not much,' her sister replied. She continued to read
the newspaper. 'Wait a minute!' she said. 'This is a
strange story.' They read the story together. It said:

GHOST SEEN AGAIN. A fisherman named Toinbe said that he saw a ghost at the old wharf. Toinbe was coming home from the beach late on Tuesday night, when he heard strange music coming from the wharf. Then he saw a strange green light 5 *moving along it. It was a ghost with large dark eyes.*

Toinbe was very frightened when he saw the ghost. He said that he would never go near the wharf again at night. 10

Several other people say they have seen the ghost at the old wharf.

Who is Toinbe?

'That's exciting news,' Serina said. 'I wish I could see the ghost.' 15

'I don't want to see any ghosts,' said Piren. 'I don't mind reading about them in books, but I don't want to see any.'

'Ghosts don't hurt you,' Serina told her. 'They only frighten you.' 20

'I don't want to be frightened,' Piren answered. 'Let's go and buy the fish for Mother.' They walked to the market.

At the market, the girls saw fish laid on small tables. They chose three big ones and paid the fisherman. 25 Then Serina had an idea.

'Where can I find Toinbe the fisherman?' she asked the man who had sold them the fish.

'I don't know a fisherman named Toinbe,' he answered. 30

'Perhaps he comes from a different village,' Serina said. But the man shook his head.

'I know all the fishermen near here,' he said. 'I'm certain that there isn't one called Toinbe.' The girls thanked the man and walked away with their fish.

'Perhaps the newspaper used the wrong name,' said
5   Piren.

'Yes, perhaps,' Serina agreed. The girls went home to their mother.

The wharf looks safe

In the afternoon, they decided to go for a swim. They
10   put some food in a bag, got on their bicycles and cycled to a beach near their home.

The water was warm and the two girls swam and splashed happily. Then they went to look at the small fish in the pools near the beach. They tried to catch
15   some but the fish were too quick.

'I'm hungry,' Serina said. 'Let's eat.' They sat under a tree and ate some fruit.

Far away, they saw the old wharf. It was like a bridge going straight out to sea, but of course it did not go
20   very far.   After about a hundred metres it just stopped.

Serina looked at it for a long time.

'It doesn't look very frightening,' she said.

'It looks all right,' Piren answered.

'Let's go out to the wharf tonight,' Serina said. 'We
25   can go on our bicycles later, when mother and father are asleep. Do come with me! It will be good fun.'

Piren did not like the idea but, after some time, she agreed to go.

A bicycle ride at night

30   Later that night, Serina woke Piren up.

'Come on!' she whispered. 'Let's go to the wharf now.'

Silently, the girls dressed. They crept out of the house and took their bicycles from the hut. The door shook as they opened it.

'Shh!' Serina whispered. 'No noise! We don't want to wake mother and father.' They took their bicycles out and rode away from their house.
Piren thought of her nice warm bed. She was still not happy about going to the wharf.

They cycled for more than twenty minutes in silence.
'We'll soon be there,' Piren said.

'Yes,' Serina answered. 'We'll see the wharf soon. And I hope we see the ghost.' Piren said nothing about that.

There were some small trees and bushes near the wharf. They hid their bicycles under a bush which had big leaves, and walked the rest of the way.

The night was dark. A bird called from somewhere in the distance.

'I'm frightened!' Piren whispered. 'I wish I had stayed at home. I don't want to see the ghost.'

'Shh!' Serina said. 'Don't make a noise. We can hide behind this bush.' They sat down behind the bush and looked at the wharf. There was a small hut half way along it, but the girls could not see anyone there. It was empty.

Will the ghost appear?

They waited patiently in the dark for more than half an hour. They saw nothing. They heard the waves splashing on the beach. They heard the wind in the trees. And they heard the bird calling, far away.

'I want to go home,' said Piren.

'No. Let's wait for a few more minutes,' Serina said. Then, quite suddenly, they heard the music. It sounded like singing.

The girls looked at the wharf. They noticed a light near the hut. The music stopped and then they saw the ghost! It was lit by a strange green light and had large dark eyes. It began to move silently along the wharf towards the beach.

'Let's go away quickly!' Piren whispered. 'I'm frightened!'

'No, wait!' Serina said. She held Piren's arm. 'Let's see what it does next.' The ghost moved along the wharf. Then it went back towards the hut and disappeared.

For a long time Piren and Serina just sat behind the bush, thinking that the ghost might come out again. Then Serina touched Piren's arm and the two girls got up to get their bicycles. Their mother and father were still asleep when they reached home. They undressed quietly and got into their beds. In a few minutes, they were asleep too.

14

DON'T GO NEAR THE WHARF: PART TWO

The old hut

'Where shall we go today?' Piren asked. It was the day after the girls had seen the ghost at the wharf. They were riding their bicycles.

'Let's go to the wharf again,' said Serina. 'I want to 5 look around there.' Piren didn't want to go but Serina did. So the two girls cycled along the dusty road to the wharf.

They hid their bicycles under some bushes and walked on to the wharf. The boards of the wharf were 10 old and made noises under their feet as they went along. The old hut was in the middle of the wharf. It was empty. The doors and windows were tightly shut. A wire was fastened to the roof. It was joined to a tall post at the end of the wharf near the beach. 15

'What do you think that wire is used for?' Serina asked.

'Perhaps it is an electricity wire or a telephone wire,' Piren said.

'I don't think it is,' Serina replied. 'It's not joined to 20 anything. It only goes from the hut to that tall post.'

'I wish we could go into the hut,' said Piren.

The girls get into the hut

They tried to open the door and the windows, but they were all fastened tightly. The door was locked. Serina 25 pulled the handle, but it was too strong. As she took her hand off the handle, she saw oil on her fingers.

'Someone has put oil on this lock,' she said. 'That means someone has opened the door in the last few days.'

'Let's go to the back of the hut,' said Piren. 'It has a
5 window and we might be able to
open it.' Serina agreed to try this.

Carefully the two girls went to
the back of the hut. The glass
in the window was broken.
10 Serina put her hand through
the hole and pulled the handle
to open the window. They
climbed into the hut and shut the window again.

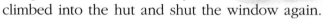

It was dark inside. There were some large boxes by
15 one wall and there was another box near the window.
Serina opened this one and looked inside. She saw a
cassette player in the box. She pulled it out and
switched it on. The cassette player began to play.
'That's the music we heard last night!' Piren cried. Serina
20 switched off the cassette player again.

The ghost is a trick

'There's something strange about this hut,' she said. She
put her hand inside the box again and pulled out a long
green sheet. There was also a lamp made from a large,
25 square tin. The tin had two holes cut in it, like eyes.

'This must be the ghost!' Serina said in excitement.
'Someone is trying to frighten people away from the
wharf. But why?'

'It's getting dark,' Piren said. 'Let's go home.' They
30 put the cassette player and the sheet and the lamp back
into the box. They went to the window to climb out.
Just then, they heard the boards outside making a noise.
Someone was coming!

'Quickly, let's hide!' Serina whispered. They crept behind one of the big boxes and waited. They heard the sound of someone walking along the wharf. Two minutes later, a key turned in the lock and the door opened. Two people came into the hut. Serina looked through a hole in the box. She saw Tom Barata and his wife.

'Hurry,' they heard Tom Barata say. 'Let's make everything ready. Perhaps we'll find it tonight. Then we'll be rich.'

'I hope you do find it tonight, Tom,' Mrs Barata said. 'You're too old to go diving.'

The diver

The girls watched from behind the box. They saw Tom Barata pull out some diving clothes. His wife took out the cassette player. She looked at it carefully.

'That's strange, Tom,' she said. 'The cassette player has been moved.' The girls looked at each other.

'Do you think someone has been in the hut?' they heard Tom Barata say. The girls kept very still.

'No. The door was still locked when we arrived,' said Mrs Barata. 'No one has broken the lock. Perhaps I made a mistake about the cassette player.' She pulled out the green sheet and the lamp from the bottom of the box. The girls smiled at each other thankfully. It was all right.

'I hope we find it tonight,' Mrs Barata said. 'I don't like frightening people with this ghost.'

'Don't worry,' her husband said. 'It doesn't hurt anyone.'

Mrs Barata carried the sheet and lamp outside.

'I've put the ghost on the wire, Tom,' she said when she came back. 'I'll light the lamp as soon as you start.'

The girls watched Mrs Barata help her husband into his diving clothes. Then Tom bent down and lifted a trapdoor in the floor of the hut. There was a ladder just below it, going down towards the water.

5 Tom Barata climbed slowly down through the trapdoor. The girls heard him as he went down a ladder.

'Good luck, Tom!' called Mrs Barata. There was a splash as he dived into the water below, then silence.

Mrs Barata looked down
10 through the trapdoor.

'Help me!'

Minutes passed. The girls were afraid to move as they waited behind the box. Mrs Barata went outside to light the ghost lamp and came back. She sat down
15 and waited for Tom to return. A few minutes later, there was another splash as he came up for air.

'Have you found it, Tom?' she called.

'No, I can't see it,' he answered. 'I'll go down again in a minute or two. It's very cold down there tonight.'
20 He dived again.

Suddenly there was a cry from below.

'Help me! Help me!' Tom Barata shouted. 'I can't move my legs! I need help!'

'What can I do?' Mrs Barata cried. 'I can't climb down the ladder.'

'Get a rope or something,' her husband shouted. 'I shall drown! You must help me!'

'There's no rope here,' Mrs Barata screamed.

'Help me!' her husband cried. 'I'm going down! Get a rope and …' There was a splash from below, then silence.

'Tom! Tom!' Mrs Barata called. But there was no answer from below. There was only the noise of the waves as they splashed against the ladder.

Will Tom drown?

Tom Barata had disappeared under the water. Serina and Piren ran from behind their box to the trapdoor. Mrs Barata was very surprised to see them.

'What are you doing here?' she asked.

'We'll tell you later,' Serina said. 'Your husband needs help down there.'

Quickly, the girls climbed down the ladder. Piren waited at the bottom of the ladder and Serina dived into the water.

She came up a few seconds later, opened her mouth for air and went down again. A few seconds later, she came up again. This time, she was pulling Tom Barata with her.

'Give me your hand!' she called. Piren leaned down and held the old man's arm. Serina held him from below so that his head was above the water. His mouth moved. Serina saw poor Mrs Barata looking through the trapdoor.

'He's alive,' she said. 'He'll be all right.'

The girls waited until Tom was strong enough to climb up the ladder into the hut. Mrs Barata put a warm blanket around him and gave him a hot drink. Soon
5 Tom was much better.

Tom Barata's story

The girls sat on boxes and waited for him to speak. Mrs Barata closed the trapdoor with a loud bang.

'You won't dive again, Tom Barata,' she said. The old
10 man agreed.

'But what were you diving for?' Piren asked.

'I was diving for gold,' he answered.

'Tell the girls the story, Tom,' his wife said.

'Well, about thirty-five years ago, I worked near here,'
15 the old man began. 'I was a gold miner. I worked hard for about five years, but I found very little gold. Then one day, I found a lump of gold as big as my hand. I dug again and discovered two other lumps that were almost as big. I could have sold them for a lot of money.
20 I decided to send the gold to the bank in Port Moresby. I put the lumps into a strong box and carried it to the wharf. The men on the wharf put the box of gold into a cargo-net. Then the crane lifted the net up to the ship. Just then, there was a shout and someone pointed to
25 the sky. I looked up and saw six Japanese planes flying towards the ship.'

'What were they doing?' Piren asked.

Gold at the bottom of the sea

'It was war-time,' Tom Barata said. 'They were coming
30 to attack the ship! When the planes started dropping their bombs, everyone ran away. My gold was still in

the cargo-net, hanging
above the water. There were
no sailors to pull the net in, because
they had all run away. Then one of the planes dropped
a bomb quite close to me. I don't remember anything   5
after that. When I woke, I was in the hospital.'

Mrs Barata went on with the story.

'The crane was destroyed,' she said. 'The gold went
to the bottom of the sea. Tom had to go away because
the Japanese were coming. But he decided to return   10
after the war and look for his gold.'

'That's what we were doing tonight,' Tom Barata
explained. 'We used the ghost to frighten people away
from the wharf. If people knew I was looking for my
gold, they would look for it too.'   15

'So the story about Toinbe the fisherman wasn't true?'
Serina said.

'No, it wasn't true,' the old man replied. 'I printed it
in the newspaper to frighten people. But it doesn't
matter now. I'll never find the gold now.'   20

Some things are better than gold

'No, I don't think you will find the gold,' Serina told him gently. 'This is not the same wharf that was here thirty years ago. When the Japanese came, they completely destroyed the old wharf. The Government built another wharf after the war. This is it. It looks like the old one but it is in a different place.'

Tom was silent. Mrs Barata put her arm around him. 'Come,' she said softly. 'Let's go home, Tom.'

Serina and Piren found their bicycles and walked with the old man and his wife as far as the door of their shop.

'Thank you for saving my husband's life,' Mrs Barata said.

'Yes, thank you, girls,' Tom Barata added. 'I shall not dive for gold again. We have many friends in this town. My business is very successful and people like the newspaper. These things are better than gold.' He shook each girl's hand.

Serina and Piren left Mr and Mrs Barata and cycled home to change their wet clothes.

QUESTIONS AND ACTIVITIES

CHAPTER 1

*Who did these things? Choose from: **Zain**, **Abu**, or **Abu and Ali**.*

1 _____ found a good hiding place inside a hollow tree.
2 _____ said in a deep, slow voice that he was the Talking Tree.
3 _____ noticed marks in the mud near the foot of the tree.
4 _____ used pieces of wood to make a ladder.
5 _____ poured fruit juice and oil over Zain's head.

CHAPTER 2

Which of these sentences are true and which are false? What is wrong with the false ones?

1 Harun was no taller than the girls in Primary Two.
2 The other children never asked Harun to play.
3 Noor's father asked Harun if she had seen Noor.
4 Suddenly, Harun remembered the old pool.
5 The men saw Noor lying at the bottom of the deep well.
6 Harun was too big to go down the narrow well.
7 Harun tied to other end of the rope around Noor.
8 Harun's father said he was very angry with her.

CHAPTER 3

Put the sentences in the right order to say what happens in this story.

1 He made a mistake and didn't mix oil with the petrol.
2 A man in the boat asked them to fill a tank with petrol.
3 Sam and Horace were busy painting an old boat.
4 Sam said that the man's boat would not go very far.
5 Horace took the man's tank away to fill it with petrol.
6 They saw a small motor-boat coming down the river.

CHAPTER 4

Put the letters of these words in the right order to say what happens in the story. The first one is 'village'.

In the (1) **gallive**, the (2) **gnwided safet** had begun. Sharif thought she was (3) **rymignar** Ahmad, but it was (4) **elyral** Hassan who sat (5) **seebid** her. Suddenly, she (6) **ictenod** something. She held Hassan's arm (7) **gythlit** and (8) **macresed** that he was Hassan. She (9) **dabneg** her head on the (10) **drogun** and asked where he was (11) **dhinig** Ahmad.

CHAPTER 5

*Use these words to fill in the gaps: **fountain, collect, Emperor, impossible, beggar, returned, dry, necklace, palace, knew.***

An old (1) _____ walked into the (2) _____ and told the (3) _____ that he could make a (4) _____ of water drops. He needed a princess to (5) _____ the water drops for him. The princess ran to the (6) _____, but when she (7) _____, her hands were (8) _____. Then she (9) _____ that it was (10) _____ to do what she wanted.

CHAPTER 6

Choose the right words to say what happens in the story.

Sui-ming's chickens did not (1) **lay / sell** many eggs. The man at the Town (2) **Hall / House** told him he should buy the right (3) **food / fence** for his chickens. He said he should get some better (4) **chickens / vegetables**, too. Soon Sui-ming had enough eggs to take to (5) **work / town** every day. He didn't have time to be (6) **happy / unhappy** any more.

CHAPTER 7

There is one mistake in each of these sentences: correct the mistakes to show that Wai-choy was telling the truth.

1   The note Wai-choy threw was written with a pencil.
2   Wai-choy was writing his answers with a pen.

3 Wai-choy said he had a pen and a pencil.
4 Wai-choy had not finished Question Eleven.
5 The writing in the note was the same as Wai-choy's.

CHAPTER 8

*Who said these things? Choose from: **Nicolas**, **Alice**, **Absalon** or **Alice's father**.*

1 'Alice would be a good wife for me.'
2 'Find a husband who is rich and clever.'
3 'We haven't much time before the flood comes.'
4 'Now we can arrange to run away and get married.'
5 'I've put my clothes in a bag.'
6 'This is a wedding present for you!'
7 'The flood has come, and I have just finished my boat!'

CHAPTER 9

Put the words at the end of each sentence in the right order, to say what the story is about.

1 The spacemen   [box] [to] [managed] [the] [open].
2 They saw their   [in] [and] [flying] [jumped] [saucer].
3 They decided to   [van's] [through] [break] [roof] [the].
4 The flying saucer   [very] [a] [engine] [strong] [had].
5 Soon it had lifted   [road] [the] [off] [van] [the].

CHAPTER 10

Put the beginning of each sentence with the right ending.

1 Tara collected some heavy stones   (a) and moved forward with its mouth wide open.
2 Then he collected dry grass and sticks   (b) to discover where the smoke came from.
3 Next, Tara lit the grass and sticks   (c) and placed them at the top of a hill.

4   The dragon smelt the smoke and slid up the hill

5   It saw Tara at the top of the hill

6   Tara pushed the hot stones into the dragon's mouth.

(d) so that it roared in pain and rolled down the hill.

(e) and put these around the stones.

(f) and soon they were burning fast.

CHAPTER 11

The letters in these words are all mixed up. What should they say? The first one is 'ordered'.

The teacher (1) **dreedor** everyone to get under their desks. (2) **dunydelS** there was a crash, louder than (3) **herntud**. The (4) **matynide** had (5) **poddexle**. The (6) **lubindig** shook, (7) **scritupe** fell down, windows (8) **ledtrat**, and doors (9) **strub** open. (10) **yuLlick**, no one was hurt.

CHAPTER 12

Choose the right names to fill in the gaps: **the headmaster, the audience, Neri, Grace, Peter, Wili.** *You will need to use some names more than once.*

At last it was (1) _____'s turn to play. (2) _____ switched on the cassette player. (3) _____ pretended to play. (4) _____ thought (5) _____ was a wonderful piano player. But then the music stopped, and (6) _____'s voice came from the cassette player, and then (7) _____'s. (8) _____ looked very surprised. (9) _____ was staring at him. (10) _____ was looking at (11) _____. (12) _____ roared with laughter.

CHAPTERS 13 & 14

Two sentences in each paragraph have mistakes in them. Put them right to say what really happened.

1   A farmer named Toinbe heard strange music coming from the wharf. He saw a ghost with large green eyes. Serina and Piren decided to see the ghost for themselves.

2 The two girls climbed into a boat on the wharf. They saw Mrs Barata put the 'ghost' on the wall. Then they saw her dive down into the sea.

3 Mr Barata hurt his arms and could not swim. Serina and Piren pulled him out of the water. Mr Barata told them he was looking for gold he had lost in a storm.

FRANKLIN PIERCE COLLEGE LIBRARY

00083560

Grade 1

Alice's Adventures in Wonderland
Lewis Carroll

The Call of the Wild and Other Stories
Jack London

Emma
Jane Austen

Jane Eyre
Charlotte Brontë

Little Women
Louisa M. Alcott

The Lost Umbrella of Kim Chu
Eleanor Estes

Tales From the Arabian Nights
Edited by David Foulds

Treasure Island
Robert Louis Stevenson

The Jungle Book
Rudyard Kipling

Life Without Katy and Other Stories
O. Henry

Lord Jim
Joseph Conrad

A Midsummer Night's Dream and Other Stories from Shakespeare's Plays
Edited by David Foulds

Oliver Twist
Charles Dickens

The Talking Tree and Other Stories
David McRobbie

Through the Looking Glass
Lewis Carroll

The Stone Junk and Other Stories
D.H. Howe

Grade 2

The Adventures of Sherlock Holmes
Sir Arthur Conan Doyle

A Christmas Carol
Charles Dickens

The Dagger and Wings and Other Father Brown Stories
G.K. Chesterton

The Flying Heads and Other Strange Stories
Edited by David Foulds

The Golden Touch and Other Stories
Edited by David Foulds

Gulliver's Travels — A Voyage to Lilliput
Jonathan Swift

Grade 3

The Adventures of Tom Sawyer
Mark Twain

Around the World in Eighty Days
Jules Verne

The Canterville Ghost and Other Stories
Oscar Wilde

David Copperfield
Charles Dickens

Fog and Other Stories
Bill Lowe

Further Adventures of Sherlock Holmes
Sir Arthur Conan Doyle